Happy Trails

Happy Trails

A LITTLE BOOK OF TRAVEL TIPS

RUNNING PRESS

PHILADELPHIA · LONDON

A Running Press® Miniature Edition™
© 2002 by Running Press
All rights reserved under the Pan-American
and International Copyright Conventions
Illustrations © Andrew Selby
Printed in China

Library of Congress Cataloging-in-Publication Number 2002100731

ISBN 0-7624-1384-0

This book may be ordered by mail from the publisher.
Please include $1.00 for postage and handling.
But try your bookstore first!

Running Press Book Publishers
125 South Twenty-second Street
Philadelphia, Pennsylvania 19103-4399

Log onto www.specialfavors.com to order Running Press® Miniature Editions™ with your own custom-made covers!

Visit us on the web!
www.runningpress.com

CONTENTS

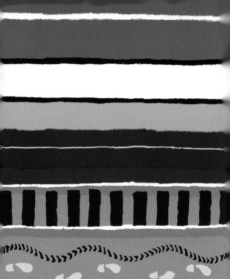

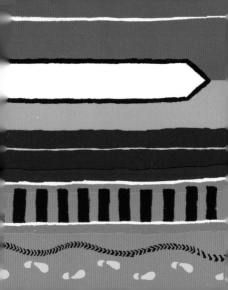

INTRODUCTION

BAD CASE OF CABIN FEVER? Got a business trip coming up? Family vacation on the horizon? Whether you're a seasoned traveler or are simply preparing for your first excursion beyond the city limits, a little travel savvy goes a long, long, way. Your moment in the sun (or snow or rain!) will provide memories for years to come. Take along a tip or two, and make those memories something to remember with a smile. Be intrepid! Be adventurous! But be prepared.

PACKING

PACKING: IT'S A SCIENCE—but a task well worth mastering before you leave. What you take with you can make or break your vacation. Comfort, durability, and appropriateness are key. Trotting around the Louvre in shoes you've never worn is not a good idea. Think rationally—you will always bring back more than you take with you. Before you pack four or five of the same item, consider the possibility of hand washing a few things while you're away. Once your clothing is in order, consider adding the following items:

BASIC PACKING CHECKLIST

Camera & film

Earplugs

Travel alarm clock with fresh batteries

Deck of cards

Sunglasses

First aid kit

Books (guidebooks and some
   paperback reading)

Sunglasses
Antibacterial wipes
An inflatable pillow
Small travel umbrella
A light compact raincoat
Hand-washing laundry detergent
     & clothesline
A durable, versatile hat
Small flashlight with fresh batteries

THE ART OF PACKING

Your suitcase will endure more
rigors on the road than your
dresser ever will. Neatly folding

your clothes in a suitcase or bag will result in creasing and crumples. Try the following tips:

ROLLING: A technique praised by many hikers and backpackers. Essentially, you need to lay the item face down, fold back the sleeves, and then carefully roll from the bottom up. This technique works quite well for sweaters and thick shirts.

DOUBLE FOLDING: This technique really helps you condense semi-casual clothes. Laying similar

items on top of each other provides the necessary cushion more
delicate fabrics need. This works
particularly well with cotton shirts
and blouses.

TISSUE PAPER: If you're visiting
a place that requires you to bring
your best clothes, you really have
to treat them as the clerk did
when you purchased them. It's a
pain, but wrapping your best
clothes both in and around tissue
paper is the only way to transport
delicate fabrics.

Never overestimate the abilities of a travel iron—nothing that light can really "press." Hanging formal wear in the shower stall for steaming is much more effective.

MORE PACKING TIPS

- Always use a business card or write your business address on your luggage tag instead of your home address.

- It is usually a bad idea to travel in denim and heavy fabrics. The lighter the garment, the quicker the "drying time."

- Always take photocopies of important travel documents with you. Passport/Visa info, plane tickets, traveler's check numbers, etc. Keep in mind however, that your credit card number is usually printed on your plane ticket. Never flash your documents around.

- Taking electrical equipment overseas? Many adapter packages sold in the United States do not contain a voltage converter. Without a voltage converter, your adapter is useless. You will need both to use your electrical devices overseas.

- Traveling with a partner? Why not share luggage? If you pack half of your garments in your partner's bag and vice versa, you'll both have something to wear in the event of a "lost bag."

- Many laptops and carry-ons look identical. Always try to customize your luggage in case of a mix up. A simple strip of neon tape could save you the headache of picking up the wrong bag.

DID YOU KNOW?

Many seasoned travelers sing the praises of the plastic "zip" bag. Although it's wise to store toiletries and such in plastic, never store your dirty laundry this way. A few old pillowcases from home will ensure that your clean and dirty clothes are separate. Your clothes are far less likely to become smelly or moldy if stored in a fabric that can breathe.

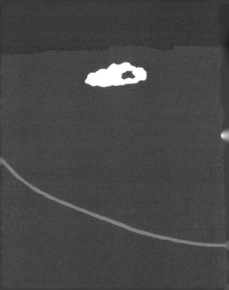

PLANES

LONG LINES? BAD FOOD? JET LAG? Yes, there are drawbacks to air travel, but it sure gets you there a heck of a lot faster. Don't forget your photo ID, your reading material, and your chewing gum—and keep in mind these helpful tips:

- It is often prudent, especially when traveling alone, to wear nondescript clothing. Never flaunt wealth by wearing excessive jewelry. Dress to avoid unnecessary attention.

- Troubled by airsickness? Remember that a seat above the wing is always less turbulent during shaky flights.

- Take a couple of herbal tea bags with you on long flights. Alcohol may induce sleepiness, but it will also leave you feeling groggy and dehydrated. Sometimes a quick cup of chamomile is much more effective. The calming effect can also be useful if you're feeling a little out of sorts, or if you're not used to sleeping in unfamiliar places.

BEFORE YOU GO

Spur of the moment travel plans? Keep in mind, many foreign countries absolutely insist that your passport be valid for at least six months (some countries request a year) from your departure date.

TRAINS

TRAVEL BY TRAIN can be a veritable cruise through lush landscape and urban skylines. The benefits of taking in the scenery without actually having to pull over, coupled with the freedom to walk around at your convenience, add to the appeal of this relatively underrated mode of transportation. Keep in mind the following tips, though:

- Technically, most coach-class train seats are the same size as first-class airplane seats. That said, you're probably going to spend more hours on the train. Bring your own small pillow and perhaps a small blanket. Earplugs are also a sensible item to bring along. Children have much more space to be rambunctious on a train.

- Take into consideration which end of the car you will be

departing the train from. Most conductors make an announcement ten minutes prior to stopping. The decision of which door will be used is, obviously, dependent upon which side of the tracks the platform is on. Use your ten minutes to prepare, as you will be expected to leave the train promptly.

- If you plan on sleeping in coach class, you may want to lock your bags to the rungs of the luggage rack. Trains make frequent stops; planes do not. Don't let your luggage leave without you.

- If you are traveling through particularly scenic areas, your train will most likely have an observation car. You can take some wonderful photographs from the observation car if you plan ahead. Reserve your seating early; don't wait until the last minute . . . everybody wants to snap that "one-time" shot.

AUTOMOBILES

IF YOU'RE PLANNING on hitting the open road, you should check out road conditions before you go. Each state has a web site and hotline that will let you know current information on highway construction, road closings, rest areas, and more. Here are some more road trip tips to help your ride go more smoothly:

- Never leave anything of value visible. Video recorders, portable CD players, cameras, luggage, etc., should always be locked in the trunk out of sight.

- Always carry an emergency roadside kit: flares, a blanket, first aid supplies, a flashlight. A cell phone also offers extra security.

- Do not travel in deserted or poorly lit places at night.

- Keep your doors locked, and close your windows when traveling at night or in undesirable locales.

- Always look in the back seat before you get into the car.

- If someone bumps your car from behind, do not stop; drive to the nearest police station.

BEFORE YOU GO

Check these five major fluid levels:
- Gas
- Oil
- Windshield wiper fluid
- Coolant
- Radiator water

GAS-SAVING TIPS

- Accelerate gently, brake gradually, and avoid hard stops.
- Do not purchase mid-grade or premium gasoline unless it is recommended by the vehicle's manufacturer or is needed to prevent knocking in an older vehicle.

FOR SUMMER DRIVING
- Keep tires properly inflated.
- Use the air conditioner only when absolutely necessary.
- Don't let the vehicle idle for more than a minute.
- Pack lightly when traveling and avoid carrying items on the vehicle's roof.

STUFF TO KEEP IN YOUR TRUNK AT ALL TIMES

- Extra coolant and a quart or two of oil
- Maps
- A full-size spare tire
- Screwdriver, flares, pliers, vise grips and a coat hanger to hold up the muffler if it falls down
- Flashlights, water, and blankets
- Don't forget: A copy of your license plate number and VIN number in your wallet in case your car is stolen

DID YOU KNOW?

All even-numbered U.S. interstate highways run east/west; all odd-numbered interstate highways run north/south.

FAMILY

IF YOU'RE PLANNING a family vacation, don't forget that planning to make the most of travel time is just as important as planning activities at your destination. Toys, snacks, games—they will all increase the possibility of arriving without having to answer "Are we there yet?" even once. Here are some more specific family-friendly tips:

46

- Give each child a cake pan
  with a sliding lid. Inside, store
  pencils, glue sticks, paper,
  coloring books, and other items.
  When it's closed, it makes a
  wonderful lap desk.

- Give each child a backpack in
  which to store all of his or her
  "stuff."

- Pack a stack of wet wipes in a
  resealable plastic bag and store
  it in the glove box.

- When traveling with small children, take along a package of outlet covers. For rooms equipped with stoves/ovens, remember to bring knob covers, or simply remove the knobs while not in use.

- Always keep a recent photo of your child in your wallet, in case you lose them in a crowded area and need help locating them.

FAMILY CAR GAMES

THEME SONG

One person hums the tune to a favorite TV show, and everyone else competes to name the title first. Whoever guesses correctly chooses and hums the next song.

MYSTERY GUEST

The player who is "it" pretends to be a mystery guest (for smaller children it can be Santa Claus or the family pet, and for adults it can be a well-known personality). The other players ask questions in turn, trying to figure out the identity of the mystery guest. Whoever guesses correctly becomes the next mystery guest.

GEOGRAPHY

Someone starts by naming a country such as Japan. The next person must name a country whose name begins with the last letter of the previously named country. In this case, Japan ends with "N," so a country that begins with "N" must be named, like Nigeria. And so on until someone gets stuck. You can also play with city names, names of rivers, names of states—whatever you want!

SCAVENGER HUNT

Before you leave, create as many lists as there are players of objects you might find on the highway. The first person to spot all the items on his or her list wins.

ALL THE STATES

Before you leave, everyone gets an outlined map of the United States and puts their name on it. The object is to try to spot cars from as many different states as possible. You can keep track by coloring the states and earn bonus points for naming state capitals.

ALPHABET MEMORY GAME

The object of the game is to find every letter of the alphabet on cars, signs, etc. You may use letters from anywhere except in the car. The letters must be found in alphabetical order, no exceptions. The winner is the first person to find all the letters of the alphabet.

GETTING AROUND

ONCE YOU'VE MADE IT to your destination, you'll need to get around. Whether you're renting a car, taking a train, or walking from one spot to the next, you should look into local modes of transport before you get there. And keep these tips in mind as well:

- When traveling by car, take full advantage of "rest stops." Your

body often needs more than a
bathroom break. Take a brisk
walk, run around—especially
important when traveling with
children.

- If you're planning on driving
  abroad, always book your car in
  the United States with a large
  multinational company. Car
  rentals in Europe and Asia are
  often three to four times more
  expensive than in the United
  States.

- An International Driver's License or IDL is usually required for U.S. citizens driving abroad. Researching this before you leave will save you numerous headaches. Who wants to take a driving test on vacation?

- When renting a car, opt for a common model that is frequently used by the locals. Request that all "rental" stickers be removed. Your rental car should be as nondescript as possible.

- Traveling alone and want to keep it that way? Always take the aisle seat on a coach or train and use the window seat for your bag and coat. When dining in a restaurant/bar, drape your coat over the chair opposite you. Antisocial? Yes. Effective? Yes.

- Always carry the phone number and address of your lodgings written in the local language. If you get lost and can't find a cop, try a government building.

CAR RENTAL QUESTIONS

- Does your rental car have antilock brakes?
- Is it equipped with dual airbags?
- Is there an early drop-off charge?
- Can you get a confirmation number for picking up the car?
- Is there a child safety seat?
- Does the car have damage? If so, ask the company to give you a report of the damage.

BEFORE YOU GO

A specific, printed, travel itinerary should always be left with a trusted friend or family member back home. If you change your plans en-route, make sure you keep them posted.

SEEING THE SIGHTS

IF YOU'RE PLANNING TO VISIT A particularly well-known place of interest, keep in mind that many others plan to do the same. Utilize the time you have, and don't be afraid to be a little unorthodox in your scheduling. You may lose a couple of hours of sleep in order to see Stonehenge at dawn, but the result will be worth it. Research is key. Know peak

visitation times, and avoid them
if you can. Some attractions
close for a month—or even a
season—at a time. Some close for
renovations. Calling ahead will
save you from wasting precious
time in line and will re-energize
your wanderlust.

HOW TO CREATE YOUR SIGHTSEEING ITINERARY

1. Research! Before you leave, have a clear understanding of a) your budget, b) your time frame, and c) what you ultimately want to see and do on your vacation.

2. Instead of choosing your vacation time based upon your favorite time of the year, check with your chosen

innkeeper or department of
tourism as to the location's
seasonal festivals and attractions.
Research what your destination
has to offer (and when) before
you book your trip.

3. Think realistically: Most
tourists greatly underestimate
the amount of travel time
involved in accomplishing their
vacation goals. Allow yourself
time for inevitable hold-ups
and snafus. Remember—

especially when traveling abroad—that when dealing with a different language, currency and customs, one must be patient and learn to adapt to a new environment. Sometimes merely changing hotels can take the better part of a day. Don't try to commit yourself to an unrealistic time frame, or you may be ultimately frustrated.

4. Geography, topography, and weather: Your map may tell

you how to get from A to B, but
Mother Nature makes the call.
If you have your heart set upon
a picture perfect shot of the
Grand Canyon at dusk, don't
be disappointed if it doesn't
happen on schedule. Set your
priorities, but be flexible. Make
backup plans for inclement
weather or traffic jams.

MORE SIGHTSEEING TIPS

- Visiting a popular tourist
  destination? Buy your film at
  home. Film prices become more
  exorbitant the more popular the
  attraction. Plan ahead.

- In many countries you can be
  harassed or even detained for
  taking photographs of gover-
  ment buildings, border areas,
  and transportation facilities. It's

always worth asking an official if you are unsure, and always heed signs that tell you whether or not it's allowed.

- Always befriend the concierge. A hotel concierge usually has a wealth of information at his/her fingertips and can inform you of both locations you should visit and areas you should avoid.

LANGUAGE & CUSTOMS

If you're traveling to a country where English is not the main language, you should learn some essential phrases to help you get around. A few choice phrases could prove to be important in the event of an emergency, and your effort will undoubtedly be appreciated by the locals.

ESSENTIAL PHRASES TO MASTER BEFORE TAKEOFF:

Do you speak English?

Where can I change money?

How much is it?

Where is the bathroom?

What time is it?

Good morning / afternoon / evening

Please speak more slowly.

Please repeat.

May I take a picture?

How much is the fare, please?

Please call a doctor.

Where is the hospital /
pharmacy?

Where is the bank?

I am an American.

What is your name?

Thank you

Numbers

LOCAL CUSTOMS & TRADITIONS

Being aware of your body language is just as important as learning your essential phrases. You should do a little research into the customs and traditions of the region you're visiting so that you don't walk around offending everyone in sight. Here are some customs to keep in mind:

- Presenting your host with an even number of flowers is considered to bring bad luck in many central European countries.

- In Bulgaria and Greece, a nod means "no," and a shake of the head means "yes."

- The "thumbs up" gesture. Again, in the United States, this gesture is universally positive; however, in parts of Africa and most of the Middle East, it is considered to be extremely offensive.

- Dropping even the tiniest scrap of litter is both illegal and considered to be highly, *highly* offensive in Russia.

- Toasting your host or anyone senior in rank or age to you in Sweden is considered to be incredibly disrespectful.

- Scratching your ear during a conversation with an Italian implies that you consider a nearby male to be effeminate.

- In Finland, sitting with your arms folded—even in a semi-casual situation—is considered to be an incredibly rude gesture.

- A circular motion around the ear in most countries translates as "crazy." However, if you're

the recipient of this gesture
when traveling in the
Netherlands, it simply means
you have a phone call.

- Crossing your fingers usually
  implies the notion of good luck
  or protection. In Paraguay, it is
  considered to be a highly
  offensive insult.

- Tapping two fingers together
  in Egypt means that you are

either implying a) that a couple is sleeping together or b) that you would like to sleep with the person you are talking to!

- The "a-ok" sign. While this may be simply misinterpreted in most European countries as "zero," in Italy and Denmark it will be taken as an insult. Never use this gesture in South American countries, because it is considered to

be extremely obscene and
offensive.

- In Japan, it is impolite to yawn
  or chew gum in public. Be sure
  to cover your mouth while using
  a toothpick.

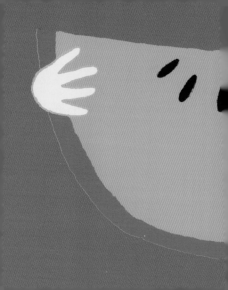

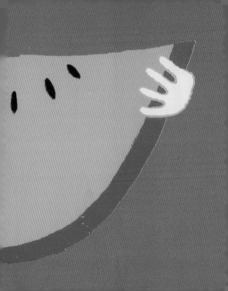

FOOD

WHEREVER YOUR TRAVELS may
take you, sampling the local
cuisine is an essential part of the
adventure. Keep an open mind,
but be discerning. Remember that
the preparation and style of food
you encounter is not necessarily
definitive of the country you're in,
but rather the region. Also take
advantage of seasonal harvest
times, which will add poignancy

to your travels. Whether you're slurping fresh watermelon in Florida, biting into a crisp Washington apple, or chomping newly harvested olives in Tuscany, indulging in locally grown food will add delicious memories to your trip. Keep these tips in mind as well:

• Modern "meal in a bar" products are usually a more nutritious snack than airport/roadstop food. You never know when you'll get stuck, so keep plenty on hand. They don't leak, they're easy to carry, and you'll also get your essential vitamins.

- Although a "when in Rome" approach is usually the most exciting and educational, think before you consider living like the locals when traveling to more "exotic" locales. Only drink commercially bottled and sealed water and resist the urge to indulge in vendor fare. Your body will thank you.

- Keep your eyes open as to where the locals like to eat. You will usually find good quality food at a reasonable price.

- Most large cities have thriving ethnic neighborhoods. Do your research, and be adventurous. The best Mexican food you ever have may be waiting for you in L.A.

- If traveling by car, buy bottled water by the case before you leave. Why pay convenience store prices if you don't need to? You could save $10 a day— it adds up.

- A portable immersion heater can be a lifesaver. You'll appreciate having instant soup, coffee, tea, hot chocolate by the mugful, anytime day or night, whether you're camping out in the woods or in an urban hostel.

- Unless instructed by your doctor, leave your diet at home. You may never have the opportunity to indulge in authentic Italian *gelato* again!

ONE LAST TIP!

ONE OF MAN'S GREATEST INVENTIONS—the clothespin—has a multitude of uses, especially when traveling. Gather your receipts, let your clothes "self-iron" in the shower, keep your chips fresh. The versatility of the clothespin is severely underrated.

THIS BOOK HAS BEEN BOUND USING
HANDCRAFT METHODS AND
SMYTH-SEWN TO ENSURE DURABILITY.

THE INTERIOR WAS DESIGNED
BY SERRIN BODMER.

THE DUST JACKET AND INTERIOR WERE
ILLUSTRATED BY ANDREW SELBY.

THE TEXT WAS WRITTEN BY NICOLA DIXON.

THE TEXT WAS EDITED BY JOELLE HERR.

THE TEXT WAS SET IN STONE SANS, STONE
INFORMAL AND NEW CALEDONIA.

LODGINGS

WHETHER YOU'RE PLANNING on
staying at a country inn, a 50-story
hotel, a tiny B & B, a rustic cabin,
or in your own drafty tent, it's
always best to make reservations
before you leave. Also remember:

- You never know who'll be staying in the room next door. A
  cheap pair of foam earplugs may
  be the only way to preserve your

sanity at night. Foam earplugs are also a great way to block out the "hum" of a flight.

- A double bedsheet folded in half and sewn halfway up the side provides a clean, fresh "sleeping pocket" for less desirable accommodations.

- A simple, inexpensive way to increase your hotel room security in "undesirable locations" is to purchase a

rubber doorstop and slip it
under the door at night.

- In-room safes are a great idea,
  but don't forget the hotel's main
  safe. The main safe is usually
  insured for a larger amount and
  could offer more peace of mind
  if you require such facilities.

- "Concierge floors" are often the
  safest place to stay. They offer a
  more regulated and dedicated
  security staff than other floors.

- The internet is an extremely convenient way to book a room. Some establishments, however, may lead you to believe that you've booked a room, when in fact, they are merely telling you that it is available when you want it. Always print out a confirmation of your booking, and request written confirmation if it is not available online.

THINGS TO KEEP IN MIND WHEN BOOKING A ROOM

- Where is the hotel located? Is it central to the areas you want to see? Is it located near public transportation?
- Are there any special rates? AAA? Family rates? Weekday rates?
- Do you have any room requests? High or low floor? Extra cot?
- Is there a restaurant in the hotel? Room service?
- Is there parking? If so, is there an extra fee?

DID YOU KNOW?

Dental floss is incredibly resilient and versatile. Use it to mend torn canvas, luggage, fix buttons . . . It's much stronger than regular thread and easy to pack.

10

★

TRAILS

50

M O N E Y

DON'T LET MONEY worries put a damper on your travels. Whether you bring traveler's checks or use ATMs along the way, you will need to plan carefully what you want to bring, how much you want to spend each day, and how you want to carry it. Write out a detailed budget, and try to stick to it. It's also good to keep in mind:

- Even though the "old" twenty and fifty-dollar bills are still in frequent circulation in the United States, many foreign banks will not accept "old" bills due to counterfeit problems.

- Wrap a thick rubber band around your wallet. Savvy travelers often do this because the friction caused by the rubber band will alert you if your pocket is being "picked."

- Many travelers sing the praises of the "fanny pack." However, a grown adult in a "fanny pack" spells "tourist" in most countries. Research your options. Opt for a more discreet and secure way to carry your cash.

THE EURO

The Euro is a singular currency currently shared by the following countries:

Austria

Belgium

Finland

France

Germany

Ireland

Italy

Luxembourg

The Netherlands

Portugal

Spain

It is hoped that the Euro will strengthen Europe's position as an economic world power. From a tourist's perspective, the Euro affords a traveler in these countries to move freely around without constantly changing money. Other European countries are expected to adopt the Euro in the next few years. Considering that one could essentially travel throughout two or three of the above countries in the course of a day, the Euro is an extremely convenient currency.

TIPS FOR TIPPING

Tipping is a very subtle custom that varies greatly from country to country. Use this general guide to help you through, but always inquire at the hotel or with a trusted local as to what is standard practice.

"n/a" means that a tip is usually not required. "I" means that the tip is usually included.

WHAT TO TIP

COUNTRY	RESTAURANT	TAXI
Argentina	10%	10%
Australia	10%	varies
Austria	5–10%	10%
Belgium	n/a	n/a
Brazil	10%	10%
Britain	10%	10%

COUNTRY	RESTAURANT	TAXI
Canada	15%	10%
Denmark	I	n/a
Finland	I	n/a
France	I (plus change)	change
Germany	I	change
Greece	I (plus change)	change
Hong Kong	10%	10%
Ireland	10%	10%

COUNTRY	RESTAURANT	TAXI
Israel	15%	15%
Italy	l (plus change)	change
Japan	n/a	n/a
Mexico	15%	varies
Netherlands	l (plus change)	change
New Zealand	5–10%	n/a
Norway	l	n/a

COUNTRY	RESTAURANT	TAXI
Portugal	10%	10%
Singapore	n/a	n/a
South Korea	n/a	n/a
Spain	I (plus change)	change
Sweden	I	n/a
Switzerland	I (plus change)	change
Thailand	n/a	n/a

HEALTH & SAFETY

WHETHER YOU'RE TRAVELING across town or across the globe, you will certainly want to stay healthy and safe. Be aware of your surroundings, try not to be an obvious tourist, and keep these other tips in mind:

- When traveling overseas, always take your inoculations seriously, and never leave anything to the

- Beach and pool areas are a wealth of information for thieves. Screaming your room number up to a friend on the balcony or carelessly leaving your keys pool side should be avoided at all costs.

- Feel free to ask hotel staff to mark your map with the location of your hotel and highlight any particular areas to avoid.

- If you see someone who requires roadside assistance, use your cell phone or drive to the nearest phone booth. Resist the temptation to stop and help.

- Familiarize yourself with the closest U.S. embassy and request a list of English-speaking doctors in the town you're visiting. This simple precaution can be taken care of before you leave.

- Always travel with a personal
  first aid kit. A vacation first
  aid kit should always include
  medication for fever, digestive
  problems, motion sickness,
  insect bites, sunburn, and
  should also include antiseptic
  cream and bandages.

ITEMS FOR YOUR

- Adhesive tape
- Alcohol swabs
- Antacids
- Antihistamine
- Antiseptic ointment
- Aspirin
- Bandages (assorted sizes)
- Bug repellant
- Burn cream/ointment
- Cotton balls
- Cotton swabs
- Digestive aids

FIRST AID KIT

- Gauze pads
- Hydrocortisone cream
- Hydrogen peroxide (fill up a small plastic bottle)
- Mirror (keep it small, in an unbreakable case)
- Non-aspirin pain reliever
- Powdered electrolyte mix (to replace lost fluids easily)
- Safety pins (assorted sizes)
- Scissors
- Sunscreen
- Tweezers

CONCLUSION

EVEN IF YOU DON'T know where
you're going, at least know what
you'll need. If you're on a once-
in-a-lifetime mission, know that
thousands of others may share
the exact same plans. Pack a little
good advice, a couple of words of
wisdom, and a sense of adventure
wherever you go. You'll be glad
you did!

Happy Trails!

RECEIPT

CHIPS

$18

TOTAL

126